101 Facts About

KITTENS

Please visit our web site at: www.garethstevens.com
For a free color catalog describing Gareth Stevens Publishing's list of high-quality
books and multimedia programs, call 1-800-542-2595 (USA) or 1-800-461-9120
(Canada). Gareth Stevens Publishing's Fax: (414) 332-3567.

Library of Congress Cataloging-in-Publication Data

Horton-Bussey, Claire.
   101 facts about kittens / by Claire Horton-Bussey. — North American ed.
     p. cm. — (101 facts about pets)
   Includes bibliographical references and index.
   ISBN 0-8368-2889-5 (lib. bdg.)
   1. Kittens—Miscellanea—Juvenile literature. 2. Kittens—Behavior—Miscellanea—Juvenile literature.
[1. Cats—Miscellanea. 2. Pets—Miscellanea. 3. Animals—Infancy.] I. Title: One hundred one facts
about kittens. II. Title. III. Series.
   SF445.7.H67   2001
   636.8'07—dc21
                            2001031057

This North American edition first published in 2001 by
Gareth Stevens Publishing
A World Almanac Education Group Company
330 West Olive Street, Suite 100
Milwaukee, WI 53212 USA

This U.S. edition © 2001 by Gareth Stevens, Inc. Original edition © 2001 by Ringpress Books
Limited. First published by Ringpress Books Limited, P.O. Box 8, Lydney, Gloucestershire,
GL15 4YN, United Kingdom. Additional end matter © 2001 by Gareth Stevens, Inc.

Ringpress Series Editor: Claire Horton-Bussey
Ringpress Designer: Sara Howell
Gareth Stevens Editor: Heidi Sjostrom

Printed in Hong Kong through Printworks Int. Ltd.

1 2 3 4 5 6 7 8 9 05 04 03 02 01

101 Facts About

KITTENS

Claire Horton-Bussey

Gareth Stevens Publishing
A WORLD ALMANAC EDUCATION GROUP COMPANY

1 A cat prowling in the long grass looks just like a miniature tiger. The cats we keep as pets are, in fact, closely related to lions, tigers, leopards, cheetahs, and many other kinds of big, wild cats.

2 People first tamed cats more than 4,000 years ago, to keep away rats and mice. Today, pet cats are called domestic cats.

3 Egyptians may have been the first people to tame cats. They worshiped cats, maybe because cats kept rats and mice from

4

eating the grain needed to make bread. Cats also kept ats from spreading diseases.

4 An Egyptian goddess named Pasht had a cat's head and a woman's body.

5 Domestic cats are much smaller than most wild cats, but they still have a lot in common. For example, all ats have a strong hunting **instinct** – although your pet kitten probably will never go off hunting deer, zebras, or any other kind of large prey.

6 When a kitten plays with a toy, it lowers its head, flattens its body, and constantly watches its "prey." Then it wiggles its rear end slightly and pounces onto the toy.

7 A kitten will start to play at about four weeks of age. It practices hunting by sneaking up on its mother, brothers, and sisters.

8 Of course, pet kittens do not have to hunt to survive. Their owners will provide all the food they need. Still, kittens can have lots of fun play-hunting with toys.

9 You should spend time playing with and cuddling your kitten every day to keep it from getting bored and to build a good relationship with it.

10 Kittens are born between 63 and 68 days after their parents have mated. The average newborn kitten weighs only 3½ ounces (100 grams).

11 Most **litters** have five or six kittens, but litters can be larger or smaller.

12 Newborn kittens cannot hear. At four or five days old, they are able to hear some sounds, but it can take up to three months for their hearing to develop completely.

15 Cats can see very well, even in the dark. Their excellent vision makes them good hunters. People used to think cats could see only in black and white. Now scientists believe that cats can see some colors, too.

13 A cat has close to 30 tiny muscles in its ears. With all these muscles, the cat can turn its ears very quickly toward any sound it hears.

16 All kittens are born with blue eyes. As kittens get older, however, the eyes usually turn green.

14 Kittens cannot see when they are born. They open their eyes after about a week, but their sight is not fully developed until they are three months old.

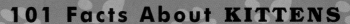

7

20 When you first get a pet kitten, you will probably have to feed it three or four small meals a day.

17 Cats are carnivores, which means they must eat meat to survive.

18 When a kitten is first born, the only food it needs is its mother's milk. As it grows, however, it will need solid food for energy and strength.

21 As your kitten grows, you can reduce the number of meals, but increase the amount of food in each one. When a kitten is about 17 weeks old, it needs only two meals a day.

19 At about three weeks old, kittens get baby teeth so that they can start eating solid food.

22 Kittens do not drink a lot, but fresh water should always be available in case they get thirsty.

23 When a kitten laps, or drinks, it dips its tongue into water and curls the end of the tongue. Then it flicks the water to the back of its mouth and swallows it.

24 Many people think they should give cats cow's milk to drink. Although most kittens and cats love cow's milk, they should not drink it. It can upset their stomachs.

25 Soon after you first bring your kitten home, you should take it to a veterinarian, or animal doctor, for a checkup. The doctor will tell you about **vaccinations** and other treatments a kitten needs.

26 Cats are very clean animals. By the time your new kitten is seven weeks old, it will already be **grooming** itself.

27 A cat uses its rough tongue to groom itself. Because its body is so **flexible**, a cat can reach most of its fur with its tongue. For hard-to-reach places, the cat will lick its paw, then use the paw to wash, for example, behind its ears.

28 Grooming keeps a cat's fur clean and separates the hairs to prevent **mats** and tangles from forming. A cat needs a well-groomed coat to keep it warm in winter and cool in summer.

29 Because your kitten will keep itself clean, you normally will not have to give it a bath.

30 Your kitten will wash its fur by itself, but its coat should also be gently brushed. Daily brushing helps remove loose hair that can form **hair balls** inside the kitten's stomach when the kitten cleans itself.

10

33 In the house, cats will scratch on the furniture or carpeting. This kind of scratching, however, does not wear down a cat's claws, so a veterinarian will probably have to clip them now and then.

31 Brush and comb your kitten from head to ail. You should comb right down to the skin – but gently. Be sure to comb the kitten's belly and under its arms.

32 Outdoors, cats clean, sharpen, and wear down their claws by climbing and scratching on trees.

11

34 Train your kitten, as early as possible, to use a scratching post. If it scratches on furniture, say "no" firmly to make it stop.

35 Cats have **retractable claws**. A cat can push out its claws when it needs them to climb or scratch and pull them back in when it does not need them.

36 When you pet a kitten on your lap, it might start to press against your leg – first with one front paw, then the other, and first with its claws in, then with it claws out. This pressing is called "kneading." A kitten learns to knead when it has to press against its mother's stomach to get milk. If a kitten kneads your lap, it is probably very comfortable with you and sees you as a mother figure.

38 Kittens will purr when they drink their mother's milk, when they are peaceful, and, sometimes, when they are in pain.

39 Kittens also purr when they want to show that they are being **submissive** and are not planning to fight or attack.

37 When you cuddle a kitten, you will hear t purr. Purring sounds like a car engine that is running quietly. Domestic cats are the only animals that purr this way. They start purring when hey are only a week old.

40 Cats can be noisy, too. "Caterwauling" is a loud howling or screeching sound a male cat makes when it is fighting over its territory.

41 Cats can also growl. Growling is a low rumbling sound cats use as a warning, especially to tell other cats to go away.

42 Cats and kittens hiss and spit when they are fighting. To look more ferocious or more **aggressive**, a kitten might also bare its teeth when it is hissing and spitting.

43 Cats and kittens make lots of sounds They even mew, or meow, in several ways. Short or long, a meow can mean many things from "hello" to "feed me."

44 Kittens like to rub their bodies against things. They rub to mark a territory with their own scent.

45 Watch your kitten to see how flexible it s. The muscles that connect a cat's backbones allow the cat to stretch and bend. So kittens can twist and roll and get into all kinds of positions.

46 A cat can even twist and turn its body in midair, so it will almost always land on its feet.

47 A cat's skeleton is a lot like a dog's, and cats have 24 more bones than people do.

48 You can learn about cats from their body language. A happy cat holds its tail high. A hunting cat's tail is low. A scared cat's tail is between its legs. An angry or worried cat flicks its tail.

50 Watching a kitten's eyes can also tell you about its feelings. When it is play-hunting, its eyes will widen, and its pupils (the black part in the middle of each eye) might get bigger.

51 When your kitten feels **threatened**, it will try to look as large as possible by arching its back and fluffing up its coat.

49 A cat that is content and feels safe holds its ears forward. When a cat is nervous or worried, it might hold its ears back to pick up sounds from all around it. If a cat is angry or ready to fight, it usually flattens its ears.

54 Although its tail is very helpful, a kitten can manage without one. When a tail is injured, it must sometimes be removed. Cats of the Manx **breed** never had tails in the first place – they are born without them!

52 When a cat is angry, its hackles, which is he fur along its backbone, will often stand on end.

53 A kitten's tail helps it balance and walk narrow paths without losing ts footing. The tail should be handled gently because it is part of the kitten's backbone.

55 A kitten's whiskers and eyebrows are very sensitive hairs that, like an insect's antennae, can feel the vibrations of things around them.

56 Kittens have four rows of whiskers. The whiskers are usually longer than the cat is wide, so if a kitten's head and whiskers can fit through a space, its body will fit, too.

57 When kittens play, their whiskers move forward to help them focus on their "prey."

58 Even if it cannot see, a cat can sense when something is in front of it. The cat's whiskers can feel differences in the way air is flowing by.

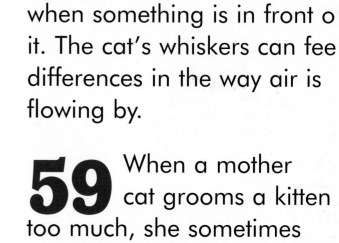

59 When a mother cat grooms a kitten too much, she sometimes washes its whiskers right off! Luckily, the whiskers grow back quickly.

60 Kittens are very smart and can be trained to do many things. One of the first things to teach your kitten is its name.

training pet cats does not take long. Often, mother cats will even teach their kittens to use a litter box.

62 If you must train your kitten, put a litter box in a quiet place and fill it with at least 2 inches (5 centimeters) of cat litter. Encourage the kitten to dig in the litter with its paws. If you put the kitten in the litter box often, it will soon start using the box by itself.

Say your kitten's name often. Saying its name while you pet it or feed it will help your kitten associate the name with enjoyable things.

61 Your kitten must also be trained to use a litter box. Even wild cats look for somewhere to dig when they go to the bathroom, so

63 If you want to teach your kitten to sit up, dangle a toy above its head. When the kitten sits back on its hind legs to reach for the toy, say "up." Reward the kitten by giving it the toy. With practice, your kitten might sit up even when you just say the command.

64 Everyone knows that dogs like to play fetch, but some kittens like that game, too!

65 Throw a small toy. Your kitten's chase instinct will make it run afte the toy. As soon as the kitte has the toy in its mouth, cal the kitten back to you. Whe the kitten comes back, it wil hopefully, bring you the toy.

66 You can also train your kitten to "speak." Whenever the kitte mews, say "speak." Reward the kitten by petting it.

67 Another way to train your kitten to speak is to hold a treat in your hand and ask if the kitten would like it. When the kitten mews, give the treat as a reward.

68 Some types of cats are more talkative than others. Siamese cats, for example, are commonly known to be chatterboxes.

69 Being walked on a leash is not natural for cats, but kittens can be trained to do it. Before taking your kitten outside, however, let it play and walk around inside with a leash on.

21

70 When a cat's parents are both the same particular breed, the cat is a **purebreed**. A cat with parents that are each a different breed is a **crossbreed**.

71 Different breeds of cats have different types of coats. Because of their coats, cats are divided into two main groups: longhairs and shorthairs.

72 Longhair cats need frequent grooming. Persian cats (above) and Maine Coons are purebreeds with long hair.

73 Siamese purebreeds and many kinds of crossbreeds have short hair.

74 A Sphynx cat's hair is so short that it looks like there is no hair at all!

75 The coats of some cats, such as the Cornish Rex breed, have short, wavy hair.

76 The largest domestic cats are Ragdolls. These cats are so relaxed that they go limp, like a rag doll, when you pick them up.

77 Some people think cats hate water, but Turkish Van cats love it. They even like to swim in it. Their name comes from Lake Van in Turkey. Turkish Van kittens might spend hours playing with running water.

78 Bengal cats also love water. These Bengals are not tigers. They are bred from small Asian wild cats called leopard cats.

79 Cats' coats can be many different colors or mixtures of colors, including black, white, gray, brown, orange, red, and cream.

80 Tortoiseshell cats (above) have coats that are a mixture of black, red-orange, and, sometimes, cream or white hair. Most tortoiseshell cats are females.

81 Tabby cats (right) can have red, silver, brown, cream, or blue hair in a variety of markings. A Tabby might be marbled, striped, spotted, or **ticked**, with light shades of color next to dark shades or black.

82 Pointed cats generally have one color of hair on their bodies and either lighter or darker colors on end points such as the head, paws, and tail. Siamese cats and Ragdolls often have pointed markings.

83 Your kitten needs a quiet place to sleep. Many kittens like

...beds with hoods, because they are warm and keep out drafts. Sleeping bag-style beds are good, too. Kittens enjoy tunneling into them.

84 With all the growing and playing they do each day, kittens need lots of catnaps. In fact, all cats sleep a lot. Even adult cats sleep 16 to 18 hours a day.

85 Your cat should wear a collar with your telephone number on it. Then, if the cat gets lost, it can be returned to you. Be sure the collar is made so your cat can get free if the collar catches on something. Some collars stretch or unclip when they get caught on things.

86 Collars that have bells on them can keep your cat from killing birds or mice. The prey can hear the cat coming. Some collars are electronic. They warn birds when a cat is about to pounce.

87 Your kitten should have a collection of strong, safe toys to play with. Kittens especially love balls and toys that dangle.

88 **Catnip** is a harmles herb that can make cats and kittens very playful.

89 If your kitten seems bored with a toy, try sprinkling catnip powder on the toy. Not all cats, however, especially kittens less than six months old, will react.

90 Do not allow your kitten outside until after it has had all of the vaccinations it needs to protect it from serious diseases.

91 When you first take your kitten outside, let it investigate for a while, but watch it closely. Later, you will be able to let the cat come and go by itself.

92 Because animals are often hurt on streets and roads, some people will take a cat outside only if it is wearing a leash. Some people never let their cats go outside.

93 Cats that always stay inside need lots of places to climb and play. They also need some grass to eat. You can grow grass indoors in small containers.

94 Kittens eat grass to help them digest their food. Grass also helps them get rid of hair balls.

95 Make sure your kitten does not chew on houseplants. Plants such as lilies and philodendrons are poisonous to cats. Keep all plants safely out of reach.

96 Your kitten's curiosity can get it into trouble. If a closet door is left open, a kitten will scamper inside to explore – and kittens love to nap in clothes dryers!

97 Kittens can be very clever and must be watched carefully. Some kittens can even figure out how to open cabinet doors.

98 Kittens see at a lower level than people do, so they will spot things that you might not see when you are standing.

99 In spite of their small size, kittens are pretty tough – but they do not have "nine lives"!

100 Most cats live to be about 14 years old, but some live longer. A Tabby in Devon, England, back in 1939, lived to be 36 years old.

101 Little kittens are incredibly cute, but they grow so quickly. Fortunately, full grown cats are just as lovable. Cats are wonderful pets. Big or small, young or old, cats are always a lot of fun.

Glossary

aggressive: showing forceful or attacking behavior.

breed: a special type of animal produced by mating certain animals within the same species.

catnip: a plant belonging to the mint family, which has a strong scent that makes some cats and older kittens very lively.

crossbreed: a cat with parents that are each a different purebreed.

flexible: able to move, bend, and twist easily into different positions.

grooming: making the body look neat and clean.

hair balls: clumps of hair that form in the stomach of an animal that cleans itself by licking its coat.

instinct: a natural kind of behavior that an animal knows from birth.

litters: groups of kittens born at the same time to the same mother.

mats: clumps of knotted or tangled hair or fur in an animal's coat.

purebreed: a cat with parents that are both the same breed.

retractable claws: sharp, curved nails on an animal's foot, which the animal can push out and pull back in whenever it needs them.

submissive: willing to give in to or back away from something bigger or stronger.

threatened: faced with possible harm or danger.

ticked: marked with bands that are several different colors.

vaccinations: injections, or shots, of medicine-like substances that help fight off serious diseases.

More Books to Read

All About Cats and Kittens
Emily Neye
(Grosset & Dunlap)

How to Talk to Your Cat
Jean Craighead George
(HarperCollins Juvenile Books)

Kitten Training and Critters, Too!
Judy Petersen-Fleming and Bill
Fleming (William Morrow)

Kittens
Carey Scott
(DK Publishing)

Web Sites

Naming Your Kitty
www.hdw-inc.com/
NameHome.htm

ETcetera: Cats
www.petcetera.com.au/
Cats/

Thinking of adopting a cat?
prince.thinkquest.org/4213/

Very Best Pet
www.verybestpet.com

To find additional web sites, use a reliable search engine, such as
www.yahooligans.com, with one or more of the following keywords:
kitten, kitten care, cats.

Index